Something Lurks It Seems

By Amitabh Vikram Dwivedi

Published by Marfa House
Copyright 2016 Amitabh Vikram Dwivedi

Marfa House
Marfa, Texas

Marfa House
Marfa, Texas

Something Lurks it Seems

Published by Marfa House

This book is a work of fiction. With the exception of recognized historical figures, the characters in this novel are fictional. Any resemblance to actual persons, living or dead, is purely coincidental.

All Rights Reserved

Copyright 2016 Amitabh Vikram Dwivedi
1st Edition

In accordance with the U.S. Copyright Act of 1976, the scanning, uploading, and electronic sharing of any part of this book without the permission of the publisher constitute unlawful piracy and theft of the author's intellectual property. If you would like permission to use this author's material work other than for reviews, prior written permission must be obtained by contacting the publisher. Thank you for your support of the author's rights.

This book is licensed for your personal enjoyment only. This book may not be re-sold or given away to other people. If you would like to share this book with another person, please purchase an additional copy for each recipient. If you're reading this book and did not purchase it, or it was not purchased for your use only, then please purchase your own copy. Thank you for respecting the hard work of this author.

ISBN: 978-1-946072-20-7

Table of Contents

Acknowledgements .... *vii*
Dedication .... *ix*

The Poems

Human *1*
Meek *2*
Lovers *3*
Tears *4*
Where's Love? *5*
Octopus *6*
Now We Are 10 .... *7*
Dilemma *8*
Lava *9*
Beloved Cat *10*
Meaning of Life *11*
A Fairy Land *12*
What Matters Most *13*
The Last Breath *14*
Parting *15*
Love-war *16*
Memory *17*
In Quest of Love *18*
In the Midst of Silence *19*
I Love You *20*
Lonely Splendor *21*
Kisses *22*
To You *23*
Rain *24*
Existence *25*
Happiness *26*
Journey *27*
Aftermath *28*
Book Reading *29*
Day Was Done *30*

Starts/Ends	31
Loop	32
Lover's Desire	33
To My Beloved	34
You and I	35
Silence	36
Interior Monologues	37
Loneliness	38
Everywhere	39
Realization	40
Whisper	41
Union	42
Mist	43
Scar	44
Forgetfulness	45
Mysterious	46
The Falling of the Night	47
Wind	48
Bat	49
Brain	50
CCTV	51
Duty	52
Meeting	53
Death	54
Inspiration	55
Lily of the Valley	56
No Man's Land	57
Love's Labor Lost	58
Natural Learning	59
Unfaithful	60
Emesis	61
Sun	62
O Life! I Love You!	63
Soldier	64
Deception	65
Broken Mirror	66
Black	67
Father	68
Anaconda	69

Woman	70
Islam	71
Mother	72
Consumption	73
Pills	74
Fetus	75
Guru	76
Hide and Seek	77
My Innocent Love	78
Remembrance	79
The Old Bunyan Tree	80
Heart	81
Speak	82
Eyes	83
Cats	84
A Child's Desire	85
Fairy! Fairy!	86
Difference	87
Fractured Identity	88
Burqa	89
Curse	90
Death	91
Ecstasy	92
Goddess	93
Happiness	94
Life and Death	95
No Love Song	96
O Virginia!	97
Work	98
Life of a Leaf	99
The Lost World	100
Valentine's Day	101
Why Should I Love Thee?	102
Hindu	103
Rage	104
Stones	105
Stings	106
About the Author	107

Acknowledgements

I would like to express my thanks to Marfa House International and its creative team, including Allison Bruning, Maria A Zani, Eve Hal, Chasity Tarantino, Lisa Pottgen and others for working on this project.

Dedicated to...

For my love Gargi & my life Aviana.
Mummy & Papa, who gave me- my life & love.

Human

Your cry remained unheard,
Like other objects in this world:
The bark of a distant dog,
The rustling of dried leaves, and
The sound of footsteps.

You cried but it didn't communicate to me.
You sobbed but I didn't notice it,
Were they addressed to me in any case?
I solemnly doubt.

I surpassed them simply,
Considering them involuntary articulation
As your other instinctive biological signs.

The sound of pain,
The sound of suffering,
Do not constitute communication in any strict sense.
Your automatic overflow of emotional energy
Thus remained unheard.

And you accused me of being inhuman,
And I was wondering-
Without using words were you a human?

Meek

I still believe she was meek-
As her first night satisfaction
Became her embarrassment the next day.

And I refuse to believe that
She was feigning sleep,
Only to avoid the clasp of my arms the other day.

Guys, laugh at me!

I came to know recently that
Her cheeks flushed red,
And her skirt rode up
While making love with my brother
When I was away.

However, she was meek again
On my return,
And whenever my hands fumbled
She blushed a lot.

Lovers

Blessed with a huge slice of luck,
Are those who can make love
Under pale moonlight,
Where their bodies move beneath
A leafy tree.

And when wind blows,
All the leaves are arranged so much so
To give a standing ovation
For their perfect union.

They bend and sway-
Backward and forward-
To perform a repetitive behavior,
Though stereotype
Yet looks novel:

    rocking and swaying
                  sucking and teeth-grinding
twisting and twirling <<>> scratching and pinching
                          head-banging and head-shaking

Making love
Undisturbed

Tears

There was more pleasure, more delight,
When in my veins blood rushed like a wild current;
And I breathed in every last ember of my desire,
Your love in my flesh.

Till at last you bid adieu
And suddenly nothing left.
Your love evaporated, and the stream dried.
A dead meat, became I,
With a blank screen and madness galore.

A true lover does often fail in love.

Where's Love?

Love just vanished.

As heat evaporates ice,
Your loving me too much did to love.

Now there is a feel of snow in the air.
The sun shines fluffy and light sleet, and
Snow mock at my face.

Had you loved me less,
It would have been fated same.

Our separation didn't require a reason-
Since love started without reason,
It ended just like that.

Octopus

Like
      O
        C
     TO
   P
   U
    S
       Your ten-
            -ta-
                -cles
     Search my body
        Your touch makes me s
                  t
                  i
                  f
                  f
     My p**ea**ks manifest my desire
L   g
  a   n
    p   i
      p   k
        i   c
          n   i
              g&l
Makes me squirm
A rhythmic
    F   e
   a   s
   l   i
  l& r
We consume; **we dine together**
Like true lovers
Satiate our appetite.

Now We Are 10

The equation is "10."
I am single and free;
And he is not more.

His presence was a burden;
A life that I passed in a den.
Our marriage was an incident;
No, an accident that occurred
As a life imprisonment
I was sentenced to.

I lived those years
As if I were dying
Day after day-
Month after month-
Year after year
But now I have won the war finally.
One is to zero,
Yes "10" is my score.

I will rejoice.
I will sing.
As I were born again;
I am free today.

Dilemma

I tread on a thin line,
Like Adam's choice
Between,
Passion and purity,
Gratification and deprival.

And you like Eve's,
Ruminates on the desperate need:
Of sabotaging your chastity
And becoming a traitor
Of your virginity.

We both are biologically conditioned,
And tread on a thin line.
Our actions predetermined and destined,
To be one and we lost each other.
Is this the only way
To find oneself?

Lava

A river of steaming lava
Is ready to blow up,
And it begins.

You move aside
And maul my weakening body,
And it flows.

You return my manual labor
Like spunk you stand;
And it pierces:
You raft in me
Often reach down and up high.

And it happens:

Yeah!
Yeah!
Oh!
Oh!
O God!

I remember.

Beloved Cat

O my dear cat, my sweetheart!
You remind me of my love.
When you are near me, I am never alone.
You scratch me with your sharp claws.
It's your way to show love; there is no flaw.
Your dark cerulean eyes like some wild sea
Where I try to fathom out every mystery.
When I stroke your back; I forsake whatever I lack.
I lose my pain, my worries, and get pleasure
When I touch your agile body for good measure.
You are always near me as if you're my heart.
You are only my cat, yet more lovable than my sweetheart.

Meaning of Life

My moving body sets out with my floating soul
In an expedition,
To find out the meaning of life.

And my life spreads its fragrance
When the wind blows;
It is an expansion.

I often touch the essence.
And a divine voice murmurs, softly yet audible:o
Your soul is still waiting for the essence.

I set off on my journey again.
For the one
Who can tell me the meaning of my life?

A Fairy Land

Early morning a miracle happened
Near to the door.
A tree in the garden sparkled
Into a thousand splendid suns.

Like a fairy tale
Dark clouds formed;
The parents' room went up in smoke.

Many things disappeared in this magic.
The children were in awe
Or perhaps they were numb,
They saw shiny fruits dripping from a distant tree.

They waited for a fairy to come,
But a carrion crow flew in a faraway land.

What Matters Most

Consider! It is a four lettered word,
No, not a matter of love,
But a matter of f@#^.

No moral law is involved,
Since mortals know how they evolved:
While syphoning the python, and
Squeezing the lemons.

Conditions are same and positioning fine,
With deliberations we seek; and
With effort we determine.

Through advantages of Earth,
The derivations of Heaven we arrive.
With timely enforcement
Man & woman become man and wife.

The reward and punishment play,
And army increases-two able generals
Bring forth soldiers of discipline.

The Last Breath

I know that you were never in love.
So you asked me, why in pain?
 What a pity, that
I languished and my suffering increased,
You simply smiled and said-
No pain, no gain.

Till my eyes had no tears, I wept.
Till my body allowed, I remained
Alive though dead long back.

A poor thing that I had to drag my body,
As long as I had the last breath.

Parting

It is a good thing that we have parted.
One road,
Opposite directions,
Cannot reach the destination.

And you left me midway;
Nothing novel, I too will leave
One day,
This home.
Beyond the grave.

Love-war

Like war, in love too,
The [S/s]tate is important:
For war it is nation and
For love notion.

It is a matter of life and death:
In one you risk body and
In other heart.

Constraints determine your moves;
Factors govern success and defeat.
You must accord with the ruler:
Commander or Heart, at all times and every season,
Cause it is a matter of life and death.

Believe your ruler,
As you have no choice:
If you embrace victory the world is yours,
Otherwise you will rot for sure.

Memory

I remember as
I cannot forget that
The goodness of your heart had burnt,
My rotten memories.

Once snakes crawled there:
Their hissing flames, and
Their venom had taken
My breath away.

I forget and do not remember now
That
That love was devoid of faith,
Which kept its pace
And haunted me
In my memories then.

In Quest of Love

Your love gives me a distortion-
It's fake; it seems.

Like the sadness of your eyes
That often tells me an untold story.

And the way your smile
Defies an expression,
As it is at all times you take it back-
So nicely it seems...as if
You were looking at my face, and saying:
'Saying nothing is not love
It is a distortion.'

In the Midst of Silence

Your silence is so beautiful;
But I wish for your calmness.
And your voice is so soothing;
But I wish for your smile.

Cause your smile speaks
A million words in between-
Your silence and your speech,
Which is a grace of god
To me.

I Love You

I love you;

Not in words but
In a world
Which is created by my words-
As love is not love,
If it remains unexpressed.

Lonely Splendor

To live alone and to be alone
May be two different things;
As there is a split between-
My mind and my heart,
Which shows:
A lonely splendor where
My shadow moves without my body,
And darkness reminds me of
The brightness of my scar.
So fresh and still deep
As if I were carrying-on and keeping
The broken images with me
To my empty home.

Kisses

I discussed roses amongst your kisses;
Though the infidel throne
Had already pierced my soul.

How could I claim nectar for those eyes?
When they reminded me of the fire of hell.

To You

Memories come to my mind
As stiff words of a half-forgotten literature
Are lagging behind.

The blank pages of my mind,
And the empty shelf of my knowledge
Even sometimes search for
Simple words that could reach your ears.

Who will throw further light?
At times I search for forgetfulness-
And to forgive the past in the last
It is 'a kind' or simply 'kind.'

Rain

Tiny drops of water
Disappears
In the shower-
There is all water in the rain.

My love
Disappears
In your love
There is all love and no pain.

I can leave this world
For heavenly pleasure,
For sure, for sure...
There is no heavenly gain.

If your love forsakes me
'Cause a tiny drop of water is not rain.

Existence

Love comes to you.
    A woman comes to man.

Life comes when they meet.

    Then:

        In the dark of night
Invisible yet full of fright
        The alluring touch and its charm
And passion has really no harm

You   up   and   crawl   you
    crawl   me,   I   up

And then come into being:

        Our progeny.

Happiness

Everywhere there is glee,
When I am with you
And you are with me.

And there is a flame
That gives me mirth,
When I see you
As I can only see.

And each fold of my heart
Takes a blissful measure, and
Gives birth to pure pleasure:
With you, in me.

Journey

Pain is the journey
That in vain
I travel with you,
As you remain
A stranger in me.

Then I start my voyage
For love again,
As it remains the only way
To be away
From you.

I reached
Far and away.
I am lost now,
And is this your gain?

Aftermath

The mourning stopped, and
The murmuring started.
Though few mourned and a few murmured;
Translated their symbols into words,
Into prophetic warnings and concerns.

Also came at the same time-
The falling and rising of tone,
The low meters of the dying.

All hopes vanished, and truth laughed-
When abruptly the doctor announced that,
"His life is not done."

Book Reading

When I open a book and read
Words do not come to me easy.
First, they break into morphemes,
And then in syllables.

Then the whiteness of the page disappears
And blackness comes into being.
With a gradual play of black and white
Comes knowledge and meaning.

Day Was Done

A dog barked,
And another dog began to bark in the distance.
Then another-
Ruff, arf, auau, bow-wow-
More dogs responded to the chorus,
And soon a cacophony of sounds echoed around.

He also barked at me,
But others remained silent,
Considering it a typical male-female stuff,
Why interfere?
All became a mixture of male-
All very male: both female and male.

Barking stopped one by one,
The workmanship finished one by one,
The day was done; the sun was set,
And noises prevailed.

Starts/Ends

This world is penultimate,
The ultimate lies in afterlife,
When the visible being collapses,
On horizontal planes,
And the ethereal breaks out its journey
To other-worldly.

Sages do not know-they are intrigued.
And all knowledge must go:
Revealed and gained-
Then the simplicity smiles
At last and journey ends.

Loop

It was a play,
A simple manipulation,
When your fingers ran parallel-
Crosswise
Or lengthwise,
And you created a loop.

But it was not a play,
Only a manipulation,
When your fingers ran parallel-
Crosswise
And lengthwise,
And you suspended yourself
Into that loop.

As a child, I know mother that-

Now
     You
 Are   Not

Living.

Lover's Desire

When I was tired,
I tried to rest
In your arms.

As pleasure my mind desired;
And your bare bosom the best
Pillowed garment to my mind.

Finally, I lied and rested
In you, and
Your arms in me.

To My Beloved

I know that
The way you love me is impossible for me; and
I know
That I am only a lover, and
Not an able worshipper.

And you should also know,
That the way you touch my soul
Is impossible for me to describe
In words.

I know as I realize
Your warmth inside me
This is my part- your whole.

You and I

What are we doing?
In between:
Between you and I.

There lies an ellipsis:
There you lie and here I lie.

And we read in between:
The meeting of four eyes:
You see me,
And I see you.

What are you doing?
What am I doing?
Between:
You and I.

Silence

Silence
Is so peaceful, so deep
And mind carves out for it.

After such a commotion
That whole day makes me mad;
Blows me away.

Then Noise
Becomes your sweet voice:
A clear cacophony.

Until another day starts;
And the next day ends.

No noise, no voice
Only silence prevails, and
I remain still.

Interior Monologues

In many ways
I see you near me,
Harvesting your smell inside my mind.

My interior monologues, and
The unending thoughts of yours
Knock at my door.

In a moment open, and
In a moment close-
The gates of my eyes,
Which placed you in between somewhere:
Where
There is nothing to forget, but
The ways of remembering you.

Loneliness

So lonely my eyes see
The way where
There is no coming back.

Back on my head
Knocks your memory,
Which fails to forget
The pain
That murmurs:
How you crushed it from your frown
To me that was a smile.

And now
Love that is still unknown,
Only a thirst remains in that part.

And
It starts raining, not from the sky
But from an island
No, yes
From my eyes.

Everywhere

These clouds in a moment air,
And in a moment disappear.

Like your smile
In a moment here,
And then nowhere.

But where the devil it appears?
In that part,
You know, there is no heart.

I fear you should hurry.
No fear!
It is not in my memory.

And forgetfulness that makes
Your presence here,
In that part
You know now your art.

How human it is to be flesh?
As I remember you least but you ash-
In a moment here, and then nowhere.

Realization

God entered into my soul yesterday.
And my devil recognized the intruder;
And stopped Him from entering the gate.

My fragile valor but not silly
Created a shadow out of my image.

To my surprise, it was He,
The one and the only whom I met
In my real time and space.

If my mind finally
Realizes it now
Not so late, then today.

Whisper

You whispered so softly in my ears;
And your breath poured love in my body.

You moved so swiftly in a way
That my blood made my heart beat fast.

You touched me so tenderly
That I felt you in my body.

Oh! I remember:

You were in me, and
I forgot myself in you.

And memories prevail.

Union

Two lips
Are closed in an effusion,
As new born buds are
Striving to become flowers.

Two lips
Are closed in a way,
As if they were lisping to
Thank my love.

Two lips
Though unspoken and unsaid,
Speak volumes as only
Few know
That every picture tells a story.

And those lips now slip my memory,
But I remember the closeness.
Rest is forgetfulness, and
From now on bliss.

Mist

Mist on the mountains is dense.
It shrouds the distant rain.

But the velvet-touch of the leaves
Chirps love, and I can hear.
You wonder-
How does it make any sense?

Come rain or sunshine,
I only want to see my love.

So I close my eyes
Only to capture the pearls.
But coming amidst the mist:
It makes my mind clouded to see nothing,
But my goddess in my arms
Oh! The velvet-touch
How can I ever leave?

Scar

Words remained in the last to soothe my soul.
Your deeds gave me a deep scar in my heart.

Still echo in your words
That sounded-"Let me live in peace."

And you reflected them in your action.

But I am unaware of that death:
I lived with your words;
And you lived with your peace.

Forgetfulness

How can I forget you?
Maybe it is possible to forgive you
But to forget is impossible.

Addicted by your smell,
I dream of you-
In days with eyes wide-open
In nights with nightmares.

Leave me, and forget me for things you know
If you have nothing to give
Then forgive me for my innocence

I pray; I beg.
May you rest in peace!
How can I forgive you?
Maybe it is possible to forget.

Mysterious

There is mystery behind your silence
Which creates a commotion in my mind.

But, do you mind?
It hurts.

Since you are nothing but scent evanescence,
In a moment in and in a moment out.

But, do you care?
As you say who cares?

True to yourself, and the self that is not mine.
All these lines must be a mime.
Do spoken words mean a thing to you?
As if you care or care nothing!

The Falling of the Night

The pitch was falling silent as noises ceased to be.
The whole world is briefly dead,
Life suddenly stopped having any meaning.
Not an isolated incident of sound occurred
During the falling of the night.

Look, how darkness raised its stature,
And old mountains shrouded themselves
Into brief interval of silence and dun.
Though a bleak private warning signaled by the light,
Yet it soon became dark by the wizard sun.

I hung my hopes for the rising sun,
As my erstwhile Sun might be sunning itself
On otherworld's beaches.
But I waited for that inevitable sun,
Until all my work was done.

Wind

The wind is rising, wetting my eyes.
That warmth-actually a waste product-
Is rather salty but necessary too,
Cause it provides me a relief.

The satisfied leaves also clap weirdly,
Trying to break that prolong dryness
Through exorcising moisture.

How vast is that ocean,
How petty my life!
My mind too conspires; wouldn't stop nudging me,
And wind rises.

Bat

Early September, it was a bit dark,
I saw a bird flying in the sky.
It was really high and steady:
I thought it was a crow.
After a while, I realized it was a bat,
And soon they became many.

I told my wife, "They are bats."
She didn't believe me.
How foolish-didn't know bats' wings-
What a pity?

I again said, "They are bats."
She resisted, they were not.
I thought for a while,
Whether with a mule I am talking too.

I looked at my baby in the pram.
Such a beauty!
Do bats drink baby's blood?
A thought flashed through, and disappeared.
I lifted my baby and pressed near my heart.

"I will protect you from everything."
I said silently.

Brain

Brain is like a prince inside a fort,
Who reins this body and its parts.
A thing intrigue lives in the skull,
Where things happen bright as well as dull.

We see, hear, smell, and feel;
Only through the brain they're made real.
Or any movements we ever make,
Remain in memory, only death can take.

So far so good the poem goes fine,
But this is not what I really design.
Good silk comes when threads spun fine,
On burial of the worms we decorate divine.

So brain isn't a prince, but a prisoner instead,
Whose colours of life depend on the dead.
When body moves and actions play,
Imprints remain and poor innocent pays.

To carry the burden of bitter blind thoughts;
To face the music and never say naught.
As a man in the chain, is he ever free?
He is in the body like a clump of tree.

CCTV

It is not a recording,
But an indelible mark on my memory.
Of a triple-X movie of
Vice and venery
Which is stored in my mind, and may
Start anytime between two gates;
There is no control.
Do not know when I will become naked
In front of myself.
My soul may insult me anytime,
There is no guarantee.
For that reason I give bribe to all three:
Soul, mind, and tongue-
So that no one will reveal my secret.

Duty

Who says that I do not love myself?
It is for my love that I went to war.

When you're theorizing your sweet selves,
In parties over wine till your love for country expired.

I was searching for that last enemy on the border,
Who is still alive, only to make your life worth living.

At home, my family's sad as things are out of order,
But when motherland is in danger, there's no grieving.

I know that corruption and intellectual bankruptcy prevail,
And few fellow men are supporting Jihadis and terrorists.

But nothing can dissuade me, nor will I ever fail,
In controlling anti-nationalists and curbing every separatist.

Meeting

When rains stop and mists clear,
Come to me and wipe my tears.
When illusions of my being human are done,
Come to me without any fears.
Those hands that once slaughtered me
On that bloody Friday,
Might find some flowers-though wild-
To put on my innocent grave.

Death

A soldier dies, but no one bothers.
They think that he gets paid for dying;
And some ideologues argue that
A man with a gun should eventually die,
While paying tribute to a terrorist
In their impressive theories
On Jihad.

Nothing new, only news
For media and viewers that run between,
Dissatisfied employees' hectic schedules
And busy housewives' soups break, and
The TRP fluctuates when
Viewers' fingers play channel switching.

And some political leaders, meantime
Speculate- how to make the death rather useful;
And some like shrewd businessmen
Become busy estimating costs per body.

The higher class doesn't give a damn;
The lower bothers about inflation,
And middle class chooses the middle path:
Investing emotions in creative writing,
And common man waits for a biopic on a soldier.

The price of a soldier increases after his death.

Inspiration

Nothing can change you,
If you lie between:
Thinking, feeling and willing.

Until senses conspire and the doer undergoes:
From states-
Psychological to physical.

It will never become a trinity:
If impetus lies supine separately,
On horizontal zones.

That is a waste:
The knowledge,
The object of knowledge,
And the knower.

If there is no union, nothing can be done.

Lily of the Valley

It stood under a tree
As if a little child were sleeping
In an old but protected lap.
When I beheld it;
Early breeze conspired too.
And it drooped under the grassy attire
Of its bearer.
Little lily of the valley!

No Man's Land

Those people over the hill,
Living a desolate life,
In their own isolation,
Residing in their small match box-type homes
Away and apart from the rest of the world.
A life, filled with misery and suffering,
Where sun governs the clock
Where darkness prevails in lives
And where there is not much difference between living and dying.
Only their moving bodies indicate their presence.
No one knows their whereabouts; they are actually living dead.
They are not considered humans.
But as every dog has its day,
Today is election; and they are also remembered.
Who cares whether they know –
The name of their country, leaders, and ideologies?
Because what matters is their votes, and not their heads.

Love's Labor Lost

Nothing was abrupt and sudden;
It was planned instead.
Like a clever magician,
You crawled my nimble mind from top to bottom,
And filled my books with arcane words,
And replaced my sounds with foreign accent.
I loved my mother tongue once.
But, you deprived me of my language.
Alas! Love's Labour Lost.
I gradually lost my speech,
As all the time I just mimicked you.
I have no link to my community.
You gave me a death,
By simply making my language extinct.

Natural Learning

We have shortened our distance-
From we know about nature to
We know nature.

We have revised our roles-
From a master of nature to
A friend of nature.

We have reconciled our relations.
Earlier, it was something other
Now it is our own mother.

We travelled a lot-
From innocent Adam to
Enlightened Buddha.

Nature! You have witnessed all.
Our fall and rise;
Our folly and becoming wise.

Now along with you,
We will grow and prosper.
We know you; we will live longer.

Unfaithful

Being unfaithful is food for my body.

It is a recipe that
I prepare for myself with utmost care.

With little lies and deceits,
I fill my soul for adventures galore
Where I party with others.

I smile seriously, and
Engulf the innocence
With my subtle moves.

It is all about living-
An art that I have developed while
Facing this world all alone.

This is how I survive.

Being faithful to myself
Makes me unfaithful.
I can't help it.
But this is what I am, a selfish being.

Emesis

Suddenly I rushed to the basin
With a bowel held tight, and
Spasmodic tides started occurring near the navel.
The rhythmic mucus sticks out from the brook
Filling my taste and smell with a sticky gel
That gushed forth finally
The deep cerulean bowl conceived.
The vessel got stained, and I got light.
Convulsive tides started now in my mind.

Sun

Sun will also rise,
When there are clouds,
Cool shower and stiff breeze,
And when there is cold and shadow.
I will also rise,
And shine my soul then,
I will write poems
Till you read them,
And my sun will also rise.

O Life! I Love You

O life! Whenever you gave me wound,
And when I bled,
I just dripped and colored your canvas red.

Whenever I was blessed with sadness,
And when I cried,
I simply shed my tears to quench your thirst.

I never forgot you when I was happy,
And when I was glad,
I gave you a hug, and just smiled.

I was never ungrateful,
I enjoyed my festivals and failures with you,
And I happily took your mischief and bore every grief.

Now, it is time to say good bye,
O life! I lack words, and don't know how-
To say: that I love you so much.

Soldier

He is a soldier, but he doesn't want to fight.
He wants to sell his weapons to buy her anklets instead.
He wants to melt his adrenaline for her adornment.

When fierce rage of winter bites his heart,
He desires for her soft bosoms for warmth.
He too wants to be a spectator of her beauty.

When his hands shake in an exchange of gunfire;
He remembers- how politicians laid their hands on her;
And how her beauty ravaged by powerful corporations.

He also remembers how greedy eyes turned her into half-dressed attires,
And now in some beauty contest she parades herself naked.
His blood flow reduces to nothing; and his cold soul torments.

He tacitly agrees to gun fire, and surrenders to death.
He forgets about the deafening sounds of guns.
He does not want to live anymore; he simply wants to die.

Deception

I cannot praise a girl:
As "light of my life,"
As "fire of my loins."*

Not anymore these nymphets are:
My Lolita and Eugenie.

If ever I utter;
But never will I compliment her?
That "You will always be my favorite;"**
"My sin, my soul."

Otherwise she might surmise
That my tongue is caressing her body.

I will select my words carefully instead.
I will say that you are my life and reason for living.
I will say that you are my rose, my flower.

No, man! Not for deflowering her.

This language is a punishment; you know?
A symbolic incarceration:
How can I make my own?

If I say I like your touch,
And I want your body:
A blend of innocence and corruption is sufficed?
Something lurks it seems.

What did you say?
Me, a follower of fetishistic cult!
Sorry, I am not.
I will prefer silence then.

Let my words not obscure my desire.
And allow my body to bespeak for it.

---

* The protagonist in Nabokov's Lolita says "Lolita, light of my life, fire of my loins. My sin, my soul."

**The protagonist in de Sade's Incest says "You will always be my favorite, Eugenie; you will be angel and the light of my life."

Broken Mirror

Butterflies in my garden-yellow, pink and grey
Used to flutter about in a wintry, sunny day,
A ray of hope used to touch their colorful hue
Spreading joy and a brightness new.
In my eyes I used to see a new zest
In a divided humanity in the heaven's nest.

Now they fight for black and white on their sides
And a piece of land for that only death will chide,
But they slaughter each other, and they cry
Till madness evaporates and blood turns dry.
Heaven became hell's gate, and deaths now play.
Flies flutter around today- yellow, pink and grey.

Black

The color black makes the white visible.
But the white makes an invisible mark-
Of evil, hatred, violence, and death-
That leaves an indelible impression on black.
And reddens the sophisticated white's history
For being unnecessary inhuman; for its absence of light
But surely white makes its false presence felt.
We cannot paint everything-black and white.
Besides, there is a human rainbow colorful bright.

Father

He came to me
We slept under the same roof,
I heard his breathing, snoring and other reptilian sounds.
It seemed to me
He was tired of his life,
The life had quenched up his last red drop.
The empty sap was obvious from his sullen eyes.
He got up early in the morning
A casual sign that he was living
He waited for leave-taking.
He awaited a long
The left note said:
"My dear son-take care of yourself
You've lots of things to see,
Before I see you off."
He was not thirsty from his life,
But he hadn't waited for leave-taking,
As it seemed to me.
I heard his parting, his going
And he didn't come to meet me again.

Anaconda

The cable men struggled with an Anaconda,
They unrolled and released it from the winch
And spread a new area network.
Some are poisoned by its vibes
And the rest are planning to taste the venom.
The Anaconda, partly resting and half dying,
Finds its coffin under the dark black lake.
And our lives start; we move in the air
We talk on the burial of Anaconda.

Woman

My history is a story of long-suffering.
I suffered anguish, attack, and condemnation.
My story is a tale of survival.
It tells that I survived.

From one era to another-
From one generation to another-
From a decade to another-
And you are born to see my persecution.

Your history is not sincere.
Your story is false.
All politeness is mere cruelty.
All respect is only hypocrisy.

Your blood-stained index finger
Indicates me as a weaker sex;
Your lip service pays tribute to my sexuality.
You regard me as a sex object.

I asked many questions.
But all remained unanswered.
When I talk of feminism, you nauseate.
When I speak of equality, you show your muscle.

You are rational; I am emotional.
When I demand for my rights, you say it's wrong.
You are strong; I am beautiful.
But these beauty contests & compliments won't end my suffering.

I am not tired of suffering.
I am also not frightened.
My past witnessed, my sitting idly.
But it is not the end.

I will not stop questioning.
I will not prefer sleeping.
I will always raise my voice.
I am still alive.

Islam

I feel insecure when your look becomes a gaze,
And you stare at my beard.
I feel shy when your potent voice calls me "circumcised"
I reason why? Your equation starts with:
"Every Muslim is not a terrorist but why all terrorists are Muslims."
I only cry when "a call for prayer" from a distant mosque becomes
"JIHAD for you."
I stop thinking when you think
"Islam is a terror."
In my prayer, I silently say:
'Allah-o-Akbar'*
"I am human first, and love all human too."

---

*- God is great.

Mother

O Mother! Wipe your eyes as your son is alive.
Don't think of death as poor mortals do.
Remember, you are not only a mother but a daughter too.
And we all are paying a debt too and we do,
To our beautiful country who seeks life
In the veins of your son and in our blood.
We live and die in Her arms, and reborn in Her bosom.
O Mother! Don't think of life as wretched mortals do.
There is a life when we die for our land,
God embraces us and keeps us in his hands.
As we live only for our country,
Wipe your eyes as I will never die as poor mortals do.

Consumption

The man sinks inside the labor.
He tries to float inside the ocean.
Stillness lies and life begins.
Earth has lots of life to give,
But he only after perceives.
Time lies in bed and he realizes later.
The determined days,
The countless nights,
In minutes of floating and sinking of millions,
But he counts his move and dives in further.

Pills

It was all myth as I recalled…
A snake in a human skin,
Often…reminded me
The archery of Sagittarius.
Crawling in zigzags on the wet ground
Leaving no signs of movements,
But…
Spitting here and there deadly venom.
It was all myth, but it came true
The deadly venom made the earth sterile,
Nothing remains but the venomous end.

Fetus

I am living, or maybe dying
Inside your overprotected womb
How can nature be so cruel?
Or should I blame your reckless nurture?
O Mother! Are you deaf to my damaged blood clots?
Your spicy appetite makes me bleed,
Your convulsive moves uprooted my seeds
Inside your circle-your semblance
And, to my best knowledge, and to tell you the truth
I am not living, but dying.

Guru

What you preached
That's my neighbor "Mohammad" now becomes a stranger.
What you sermonized
That other religions now seem atheistic,
What was that blessing
Which changed my God with you?
You changed my faith,
You changed my friends,
You changed my God,
Now you are changed.
You are defeated
By a carnal desire
And blackened your reputation.

Hide and Seek

The continuous flow of words
As different masks on the same soul
Always shroud the truth-the old dusty stuff.

Flow seems clear as the semblance of any crystal
Soul deceives the absolute and our eyes perceive
Nothing but always our truth.

So many truths are born
The flow of lie remains intact,
We do not change
But crowd our faces with the newborn infant,
With so many faces
With so many souls.

My Innocent Love

My innocent love
Tries to find its ways to be with you
If ever it pines that is for you.
Sometimes it offers- a cup of coffee,
Only to see the curves of your lips,
That insatiable look you always overlook.

My innocent love-remains unspeakable
If ever it pines to wonder over your tawny softness.
Now I realize why I love coffee so much
But every counted mug has its own bitterness.

You think me immature-my poor love
It doesn't offer big mouth, and empty dreams.
If ever it begs that is for a smile, or a look,
Now I know why my love is not innocent but poor
Because as you frankly say - "I hate beggars".

Remembrance

I remember you
When it rains.
When the sun shines
When leaves fall from the trees
When bushes are coming into leaf.
I also remember you
When my eyes get wet
When my sun is set.
When I remember that you left me alone
And when memories come into life.
I remember you all the time
'Cause I cannot forget you.

The Old Bunyan Tree

Mist on the mountain
Reminds me of my home,
That was lost in the mists of time.
I used to rest there
Under the old Bunyan tree.
The cold breeze happened to caress my cheeks
I was carefree then but was very contented.
Now I live in luxury where no trees are around.
A concrete-jungle surrounds me.
It tries to smother me.
I find it hard to breathe in.
Now I am cold and pensive.
What a gain after a loss!
I have gained many things-
Money, status, and blood-pressure
I have gained stature.
But I have lost, "the old Bunyan tree"
I see everything is blurred
Through the mist of smoke,
In the mist of tears.

Heart

Inside the heart
The tree grows,
And the palpitating sounds like the beat
Stirs my mind and the resonance meet.

Inside the heart
The blood flights,
With the force in that land
Far from the earth on which we stand.

Inside the heart
In that part,
Is a small but a precious thing
Which secure the so-called feeling.

Inside the heart
Away and apart,
Sits in some hidden corner a dove
Which to my knowledge is love.

Speak

Her eyes said to my talkative tongue.
But that garrulous silence created-
A commotion in my mind.
In my imagination I thought of her image.
Her solid head was in my tender arms,
That was faithless like her weak hair,
That remained-the waste hair, and my waste love-
When she removed her head.
Then she said, "Listen!"
And she put her tender head on my solid heart.
I was silent but her eyes talked-
"Speak! Why are you silent?"
My silent tongue moved, and
I said, "Come, let's go."
We parted silently,
We said goodbye.

Eyes

Redness comes into her eyes
And two pearls drop down from them,
When she hears that I am leaving
I catch the wetness from her cheeks.
She closes her eyes for a moment and then opens
I can see the tiny red veins in her eyes
Like streets which is lighted by halogens.
I recall
Our walking, laughing and talking,
All past in the last
And now I am leaving,
She wants to say something
But her dry tongue refuses to say.
Her wet eyes say
Hold me and don't go,
And redness comes into my eyes.

Cats

One fine day, a miracle happened.
The cats got the knowledge of language, and
They started eavesdropping on humans.
They were always around.
In the parlors, homes, and offices,
They started smelling fishy.
Their kittens were surprised-
"Why mamma is without fish these days."
Even surprisingly like humans,
The kittens wanted to know the name of their fathers.
A lonely sex-kitten gave birth to a child in a brothel.
No tomcat wanted to take the responsibility.
Earlier cats used to play-Tom and Jerry.
Now they are interested in Tom, Dick, and Harry.
They are not satisfied with, "three different names."
They are searching for religions and family names.
The other day a religious cat was praying:
"O God! Save me from feline, and blessed me human."
What a pity! They are no more cats.
The language corrupted them, so did human.

A Child's Desire

I need my Mom and Dad's love
I am not a kid but a small dove,
With a tender mind and an innocent heart
To tear me apart is not a good start.
I need you both to stand by my side
Please live together and don't you fight,
I love your cuddle and your kiss
A sweet union, which I almost miss.

Fairy! Fairy!

Fairy! Fairy! Will you marry me?
I love you so much as you can see.
I will give you my chocolate, I will give you my bed.
I will give my sweet cake, whenever you were sad.
Fairy! Fairy! Will you marry me?
I love you so much as you can see.
We will dance together on a rainy day.
We will play in a pond what do you say?
Fairy! Fairy! Will you kiss me?
I kiss you on your cheeks as you can see.
You can play with my motor car, and my engine too.
You can be my best buddy if you love me too.

Difference

Prologue

He doesn't know the difference between two phonemes: [p] and [ph]
He doesn't know the reason: why should he know the difference?
But he recalls: how often he felt humiliated, and
Insulted in his village school.

Dialogue

He remembers his teacher used to say:
"Learn your English lessons, first!"
"They give us money to learn their language."
"Don't bother about your native tongue."
"Nothing, you will get from this language,
Which cannot make a difference between two phonemes."
How can he forget when his teacher shouted at him?
"You weak; dumb head! Why do you stammer?"
"Learn this difference and prove yourself."

Epilogue

He also remembers when his teacher praised him.
"Good, nice! Now you have learned the difference."
"Now, you can tell the world about our exploitation,
In their language, in English."

Fractured Identity

I am a woman, an Indian woman.
No, not an upper caste Indian woman,
But a lower caste, dalit woman.

Power is contested on my body.
Politics is playing with my rights.
People are prejudiced to my freedom.
Perhaps they want to make me less human.

Sometimes, I am not allowed to hoist the national flag.
At times, I am forced to drink urine, and cow dung.
Often, I am assaulted and murdered in remote villages.
Because I am an Indian dalit woman.

Recently, few disrobed me at a city-juncture.
I barely escaped being raped, but how long?
They said, "a dalit woman cannot dress new in clothes."
O God! I wish I had a better life somewhere else.

Do they hear my cries or it is just a clink?
Soon forgotten over discussing feminist issues
In conferences, over expensive wines and dinners
Leaving my withered soul with its fractured identity.

Burqa

Since she refused to her daily suppression,
That burqa couldn't witness her assassination.
She only demanded little light and books.
No sinful act actually she undertook.
They singled her out as there was no forgiveness,
And soon they got back to their sinking business.
They used their guns and shot her in daylight.
But things only happen when God decides.
She passed her exam against that death;
And proudly became a voice of other oppressed.
Like a shining star for every wandering bark.
She became a light for woman in the dark.
No veil can now hide her face divine.
Nor any burqa will ever shadow her shine.

Curse

It is not in my way
To come to you,
And see what you have
A pompous face.

There are so many insects near tube-light
Green, red, yellow and grey,
I think when you burst one fine day
A swarm of insects will fly away from your body.

It is not my way
To send you curses,
I can only foresee what you will become
And what will you face.

Death

The most terrible death is:
A death of a desire in a living body,
Where being desirous is-
The only sign of living.
When consumption stops, consumption of the body starts.
Without desire, human is not human.
He is dead or divine, perhaps.
But for sure, he is not living.

Ecstasy

These apparels are mere adoration on our bodies.
Pure and naked, we bathe in each other's pond.
Like true lovers, we are just born in one another's lap.
There is no sign of dying and decay.
We do not know our religions even.
We shake, and clench our fists,
With our eyes half open, and half closed in ecstasy.
We cry for light, and
Idle tears fall as we release, they do not know-
That we want to dissolve into each other's love.

Goddess

O Goddess! You are the sweetest; you are the supreme.
Embodiment of motherhood, earth, fertility, and love.
You rule over war, destruction, death, and creation.
As a mother you bring us up, as earth in you we abide.
As a sacred female you bear fruits of love and life.
O fearless! O female creator! You also make us die.
O Nut, Ishtar, Cybele, Neith, Arinniti, Leto, Uzza!
O Athena, Aphrodite, Dione, Gaia, Hecate, Iris, Selene!
O Wata, Mazu, Devi, Shakti, Lilith, Mary, Sophia!
Lift me into your hands; bless me and caress.
I take refuge in your feet; give me wisdom and bliss.
I sing for you; in your praise only my mind awakes.
In your glory I breathe in life; in your lap I gladly die.

Happiness

She wanted to be happy.
She set-off in her journey in this world.
It was a new start.

She searched for a companion.
She married, divorced, and re-married,
And she repeated her actions twice.

She wanted to live her life to its fullest.
Meanwhile, she produced babies-licit and illicit,
Both inside and outside the institution.

She just wanted to be happy.
She slept with men and women, and
She spent many cheap nights on creaky beds.

She tasted and consumed everything desirable.
Until, she realized one day, probably her dooms day,
That happiness does not come from consumption of things.

Life and Death

"Is death boring or life?"
An old dilemma stretched my life.
Now it spreads on a lounge every morning.
I wanted an answer without picking up any.
I wanted to play safe, and thus I lived for so many years.
Without any reason, and without any answer,
I lived without death though that was not what I desired.
But as all desires cannot reach to fruition,
My resignation to life also postponed.
And I lived perpetually without any reason.
Now, I am old and equally feeble.
I cannot think of death as my beloved.
It seems to me as my daughter,
Who will inherit everything when I will be gone.
She will dispose the unwanted rags and bury that stinky soul.
But still I am not sure of what makes me live so long.
Maybe I think too much, or I am a coward.
Perhaps my hamlet-mind tosses in between life and death.
Maybe I am living no more and dying each day.
Whatever it would be: life boring or death is still unsolved?

No Love Song

Love songs, like doppelganger of a dirge,
Bludgeon my ears with its boring surge.
Earlier equation between you and me was:
Perhaps you loved me and I loved you.
Now I find no love; but a sad song,
I think whom God loves die so young.
Jaunty rhythm and trite music fade
Lyrics become clumsy, my songs are sad.
When you are not with me, and I with you,
I am counting my days which are only few

O Virginia!

I know the way I entertained you were not real.
You said, "I am an archer."
I pretended your virginity- the fall from Eden.
I sensed the innocence in your reptilian moves.

When I was low you made me climb down,
When I was high you made me climb through,
Nothing but climbing I did.
An improper movement I performed with you.

O Virginia! Now let's play a game.
And you listen to my tale-
A tale of losing and a story of gaining,
A game of listening and a play of saying.

I heard my victory in losing myself.
You sensed my defeat in your smile.
But there was a cruelty on the corner of your lips.
That said, "I lost nothing but your love."
But you only lost yourself.

Work

She works too.

A mother of two,
And a woman of someone.

She shares her body to everyone.
She works for her body,
Or, her body works for her.
She does not know.

She knows that there are bills to be paid.
And she has to fill the belly those who depend.

She also pays for being permitted,
For work, to an agent-cum-husband,
Who needs regular spirits and mutton
And his bodily share too.

People pay price, and she sells each day.
And gets a prize of being a woman.

Life of a Leaf

It burst (out) from the stem
Like a red spot on girls' skin.
A flat, thin body lay bare in light;
And changed its attire-
Brown, crimson and green-
And got maturity in its teen.
In monsoon, it bathed in rain.
In winter, dew drops gave it crystal tan.
In summer, it sweated heavily.
In autumn, it shed prematurely,
Only to pay homage to the tree.
Finally, a dried skeleton crushed by thousands,
Put this little leaf's existence to an end.

The Lost World

What happened to the world; clouds shed no rain?
No tongue speaks a word; and every hope is faint.
Decency is degraded; every equation has changed.
Humility has become vanity; and all colors fade.
Sincerity is now boring; frivolity is so cool.
If you are honest then you're the biggest fool.
People are lost; new machines are found.
No one listens even how loud is your sound?
Criminals replace heroes; a lewd remark is wit
On each virtuous lip, sensuality always sits.
Weapons rein the city, and life is frost.
Humility is a pity; and humanity is lost.

Valentine's Day

Wintry night is neither cold nor warm.
The season of love and losing someone
Is approaching.
Evening breeze is deceitful-
Lovers become losers, and
Losers become lovers-
Between a fine blending of
I love you, and
I love you not.
Someone finds a new girl,
And someone forgets an old boy.
A mixture of love and losing is in the air.
Come;
Let us find someone
Who is not celebrating this Valentine's day.

Why Should I Love Thee?

This is not a myth.
It is a fable instead,
That tells an untold story about me.

No fire was burning inside me.
They bought my body and choked me up
With dancing shadows of phallus and with their lust.

They fitted into me; their love.
No breathable space lay in those thin layers.
My body looped, leaped, pooled, and spurted.

And they burnt, bit, stung, and sprung.
No one saw their dancing shadows.
Their ill-considered gestures-up and down-
Remained permissible, and they surpassed human dignity.

Only my body was burning.
It was in rage when they were in cold blood.

Hindu

I live in a myth.
It is not falsehood; it is my faith instead.
But I find answer of all logos through it.
My reasonable deliberations get intuitive narrations.
I know, why does sun rise; why does earth revolve?
I know why I was born; and why I will die?
I look at everything through a frame-
Narrow and limited in scope.
I know I am imperfect but my myth corrects me.
Though my words and symbols are incomplete,
Yet I chant mantras in praise of God
Which ancient saints gave me.
I am religious, yet secular.
Yes, I am a Hindu,
But it gives meaning to me,
And purpose to my living.

Rage

Generous tears came into her eyes
When she came to know
That he's leaving.

Not seeing him again
Filled her heart with furor;
And like a blast furnace
Her cry came out
Along with aggression and frustration.

This is not the first time.
Earlier too she had married, and
Her husband had gone for war.

On return he was crippled for two years,
And then he left forever.
Another soldier pitied her condition,
And gave his name to her kid.

Now he is leaving too.

Since wars are raging all around-
Inside her and outside her world;
And there is no escape,
Only a wait-who will leave first
And who last?

Stone

Two acts are different:
Hold a flat and skinny stone;
Throw it into the well.
The water splashes and the stone disappears.
But your fingers are rather skillful.
When you hold it in between
And skid it into the lake:
It floats on the surface for a while;
Then the stone breaks it and splashes.
It is not the sound that matters: slosh and slush.
But the ripples move across the body and it expands.
It is love that matters in life, than duty.
Four love lives forever in my memory.

Stings

Daddy flew a kite; daughter watched with care,
She thought that string the kite was so unfair.

Kite didn't reach higher as the string was tied,
As to put a bird in a cage there was no pride.

On daughter's request father cut the string,
Not a wise decision and what a silly thing!

The kite went higher; and a surprise did it bring,
It fell on the ground like a bird with broken wings.

The daughter became sad, and she started crying,
Little ones heart is tender and there's no denying.

Father sat beside her and held her hands tight,
That made her calm, and brought her back delight.

But there was a lesson that daughter learnt for life,
If cut down from the roots, no tree goes back to life.

About the Author:

Amitabh Vikram Dwivedi is an assistant professor of Linguistics at Shri Mata Vaishno Devi University, India. His research interests include language documentation, writing descriptive grammars, and the preservation of rare and endangered languages in South Asia. He has contributed papers to many Science Citation Index journals, and research articles to encyclopedias, chiefly with *Sage, Springer, EBSCO, Rowman & Littlefield and ABC-CLIO Publications.*

His most recent books are *A Grammar of Hadoti* (Lincom: Munich, 2012), *A Grammar of Bhadarwahi* (Lincom: Munich, 2013), and a poetry collection titled *Chinaar-kaa-Sukhaa-Pattaa* (2015) in Hindi.

As a poet, he has published more than 100 poems in different anthologies, journals and magazines worldwide. Until recently, his poem "Mother" has been published as a prologue to Motherhood and War: International Perspectives (Eds.), Palgrave Macmillan Press.

www.ingramcontent.com/pod-product-compliance
Lightning Source LLC
Chambersburg PA
CBHW061332040426
42444CB00011B/2884